The Library of SPIDERS™

Brown Recluse Spiders

JAKE MILLER

The Rosen Publishing Group's
PowerKids Press™
New York

Published in 2004 by The Rosen Publishing Group, Inc.
29 East 21st Street, New York, NY 10010

First Edition
Editor: Jannell Khu
Book Design: Emily Muschinske
Layout Design: Eric DePalo
Photo Credits: Cover, pp. 1, 5, 6 (bottom left), 11, 14, 15 (spider only) © David Liebman; 6 (top and bottom right), 8 (spider only), 9–10, 13, 17, 18, 21 © Robert & Linda Mitchel; p. 15 (ants) © Gerry Ellis and Michael Durham/Digital Vision.

Miller, Jake, 1969–
Brown recluse spiders / Jake Miller.
    v. cm. — (The library of spiders)
Includes bibliographical references (p.   ).
Contents: The brown recluse spider — Loxosceles — The brown recluse spider's body — A nasty bite — The brown recluse's web — Hunting for food — Laying eggs — Baby spiders — The brown recluse spider's defenses — Brown recluse spiders and humans.
ISBN 0-8239-6707-7 (lib. bdg.)
1. Brown recluse spider—Juvenile literature. [1. Brown recluse spider. 2. Spiders.] I. Title. II. Series.
QL458.42.L6 M55 2004
595.4'4—dc21

                              2002011011

Manufactured in the United States of America

Contents

Brown Recluse Spiders

Scientists have found more than 34,000 **species** of spiders in the world. Almost all these spiders are **venomous,** but only about 30 species of spiders have bites that are dangerous to people. The brown **recluse** is one of them. In rare cases, people can die of a bite from a brown recluse spider! These spiders get their name because they are very shy. A recluse is a person who does not like to be around people. During the day, brown recluse spiders hide in their webs. The spiders are active at night.

Brown recluses live in woodpiles, in spaces under rocks and leaves, and even inside houses. This brown recluse shoots out silk on top of a leaf.

three sets
of two eyes

Loxosceles

Brown recluse spiders belong to a **genus**, or group, of species that scientists call **Loxosceles**. Loxosceles are commonly called brown spiders because many of these spiders are brown. However, Loxosceles can also be pale yellow and even reddish in color.

Loxosceles spiders live in North America, Mexico, Central America, South America, Africa, and southern Europe. There are more than 10 species of Loxosceles spiders that live in the United States. Loxosceles spiders may come in different sizes and colors, but they all have a few things in common. They like to live where it is dry. They have three sets of two eyes. Most spiders have eight eyes. Loxosceles spiders have dark patterns near their eyes. They also have a solid-colored **abdomen** that is covered with hairs.

These are brown recluse spiders. (Top) Brown recluses are so small, you would need a magnifying glass to count their eyes. This is a close-up picture of a brown recluse spider. The arrows point to its three sets of eyes.

The Brown Recluse Spider's Body

Brown recluses are usually light brown with dark brown legs, as are most other Loxosceles. Brown recluses have a marking on their **cephalothorax**, or head, that makes it easy to tell them apart from other spiders. Their thin bodies are only about 3/16 inch (5 mm) wide. Female brown recluses are about 3/8 inch (9.5 mm) long. The males are smaller, about 3/10 inch (8 mm) long. A brown recluse spider's slender legs are about 3/4 inch (19 mm) long.

This is the actual size of a brown recluse spider. It is smaller than a quarter.

8

Brown recluses and other *Loxosceles* are sometimes called violin spiders because they have a dark brown, violin-shaped mark on their cephalothorax. The violin shape is highlighted above in green so that you can see it better.

A Nasty Bite

The bite of the brown recluse can be dangerous. Scientists study brown recluse bites to learn how the venom and the **bacteria** in the spiders' mouths work. When a brown recluse bites a person, he or she may feel a small sting. A few hours afterward, the bite looks like a pimple. The pimple may then turn into a **blister**. The blister turns purple, then black. This sore can take a long time, even months, to heal. In a few cases, people get fevers and their **internal organs** may start to fail. Some people get so sick from the bite that they die. Fortunately brown recluse spiders do not bite people very often, and serious cases are very rare.

(Left) This close-up photo of a Loxosceles brown recluse spider was taken in Texas. The spider's bite can be very dangerous to people.

(Right) See a doctor right away if you think you have been bitten by a brown recluse spider. Have an adult try to capture and kill the spider, and bring it with you to the doctor. This will help the doctor to identify the spider before treating you.

The Brown Recluse Spider's Web

Brown recluses make their webs under rocks or under the bark of dead trees. In houses and barns, they find spots far away from lights and people. They like cellars, attics, and closets. Brown recluses spin large, messy webs. The threads of the web are thick and sticky. The spiders trap their **prey** with the sticky threads. When these threads become dusty, the spiders build a new sticky cobweb. In the back of their webs, brown recluses build tunnels of silk. They hide from danger in these tunnels.

Notice that the female brown recluse is slightly bigger than the male brown recluse. The webs on which they rest look like thick sheets of silk.

male

female

Hunting for Food

Brown recluses eat insects and other spiders, even their own species! Usually brown recluses wait in their webs for prey to land in their sticky traps. Sometimes if they have waited a long time and they haven't caught anything, they will leave their webs to hunt for food.

When they catch an insect that they want to eat, they bite it. The venom in the bite **paralyzes** the prey. They may eat it right away, or they may wait a few days. Brown recluses don't wrap their prey in silk as do other spiders. Although many species of spiders do not like to live near other spiders, brown recluses do not mind sharing their space. Scientists have found as many as 150 brown recluses in one home!

These brown recluse spiders have left their webs to hunt for food. Ants, flies, and roaches make tasty meals for brown recluse spiders. Most brown recluses like to eat one insect per day. However, they can live without food for 10 months.

Laying Eggs

Most brown recluses **mate** from February through September. When he is ready to mate, a male brown recluse leaves his web to look for a female. When he finds a female, he has to make sure she does not think that he is tasty prey. He signals by touching her web and waving his legs in a special way. After mating, the female spins a special kind of web called an egg sac to protect the eggs. She will lay anywhere from one to five egg sacs from each mating. There can be up to 50 eggs in each sac.

Pictured here is a female brown recluse on her web. Females have a bigger abdomen than do males. This is so that they can lay eggs.

Baby Brown Recluse Spiders

About 27 days after the female lays her eggs, the babies begin to hatch. At first they stay inside the egg sac, where they are safe. They need time to grow a little and to **molt**, or shed their skin, for the first time. Spiders have hard outer skins that don't stretch. When they grow, they must leave their old skin behind and grow a new one. Brown recluse spiders molt from five to eight times before they are fully grown. After they leave the egg sac, the babies stay in their mother's web until they molt a second time. Then they are big enough to start their own webs and to take care of themselves. Brown recluse spiders take about one year to reach full size. They usually live for about three years.

One brown recluse mother can lay as many as 300 eggs per year. Some of the babies don't hatch, and many others die before they are fully grown. The egg sacs of brown recluse spiders are about ⅝ inch (16 mm) across.

The Brown Recluse Spider's Defenses

Many brown recluse spider bites happen when people put on clothing that has been stored in a closet for a long time. The spider has been hiding in the clothes, and it is surprised and scared when it is disturbed.

Even though brown recluse spiders have a terrible bite, they are not **aggressive**. Spiders bite their enemies to **defend** themselves. They bite only when they can't run away or hide. Wasps are one of the most dangerous **predators** of brown recluses and other spiders. When brown recluse spiders are attacked by wasps, they often can't protect themselves. The sting of a wasp paralyzes the spider. The wasp lays its eggs inside the spider. When the eggs hatch, the baby wasps eat the spider.

This pompilid wasp is stinging a spider. The wasp's sting will paralyze the spider so that it cannot run away or fight back.

A spider has chelicerae, or jaws, in the front of its cephalothorax. Brown recluse spiders use their chelicerae to protect themselves. Spiders' fangs and poison are located in the chelicerae.

chelicerae

Brown Recluse Spiders and People

Brown recluse spiders eat a lot of insects that are harmful or annoying to people, such as cockroaches, flies, and mosquitoes. The best way to protect yourself from brown recluses is to keep your house clean. They like to hide in piles of papers and other trash. They also need insects to eat. If your house doesn't have many insects, there won't be many brown recluses. If you live in a place where brown recluses are common, shake out your clothes before you put them on and be careful playing around rocks and woodpiles.

It is important to see a doctor right away if a spider has bitten you and you think it might have been a brown recluse. If possible, kill the spider and bring it with you so that the doctor can make sure that the spider is a brown recluse before she or he treats you.

Glossary

abdomen (AB-duh-min) The large, rear section of a spider's or an insect's body.

aggressive (uh-GREH-siv) Ready to fight.

bacteria (bak-TEER-ee-uh) Tiny living things that can be seen only with a microscope. Some bacteria cause illness or decay, but others are helpful.

blister (BLIS-tur) A sore place that looks like a bubble on the skin, usually caused by an insect bite or a burn.

cephalothorax (sef-uh-loh-THOR-aks) A spider's smaller, front body part, containing its head.

defend (dih-FEND) To guard from harm.

genus (JEE-nus) The scientific name for a group of animals or plants that are alike. Members of the same genus are always also members of the same family.

internal organs (in-TUR-nel OR-gunz) Organs inside your body.

Loxosceles (lok-suh-SHEE-leez) The genus, or group, of spiders to which the brown recluse belongs.

mate (MAYT) To join together to make babies.

molt (MOHLT) To shed hair, feathers, shell, horns, or skin.

paralyzes (PAR-uh-lyz-iz) Causes to lose feeling or movement in the limbs.

predators (PREH-duh-terz) Animals that kill other animals for food.

prey (PRAY) An animal that is hunted by another animal for food.

recluse (REH-kloos) A person or an animal that is shy and doesn't like to be around others.

species (SPEE-sheez) A single kind of plant or animal. All people are one species.

venomous (VEH-nuh-mis) Having a poisonous bite.

Index

Web Sites

Due to the changing nature of Internet links, PowerKids Press has developed an online list of Web sites related to the subject of this book. This site is updated regularly. Please use this link to access the list:

www.powerkidslinks.com/lspi/brecluse/